FOUNDATIONS
Understanding Prayer Ministry

Prayer Ministry In The Local Church

By Rev. Denny A. Finnegan

Prepared For Publication By Joseph L. Schlosser Jr.
Cover Design By Joseph L. Schlosser Jr.

PUBLISHED BY EXCELLENT PRESS
FROM EXCELLENT ADVENTURES!, INC
ATLANTA, GEORGIA, U.S.A
PRINTED IN THE U.S.A.

Excellent Press is a subsidiary of Excellent Adventures!, Inc. Excellent Advetures!, Inc. is dedicated to serving the local church and missional organizations. We believe God's vision for this division of Excellent Adventures!, Inc. is to provide church leaders and pastors with biblical, user-friendly materials that will help them evangelize, disciple and minister to children, youth and families. We are also dedicated to serving first time authors of Christian books and materials.

It is our prayer that this workbook from Excellent Press will help you discover biblical truths for your own life ad help you meet the needs of others. May God richly bless you.

For more information about Excellent Press, please contact Joe Schlosser at 404 - 784 - 1008 or by email at joseph@schlosser.com

---

© Copyright 2016 Dennis A. Finnegan, All Rights Reserved. No portion of this book may be reproduced, stored in a retrieval system, or transmitted in any form or by any means - electronic, mechanical, photocopy, recording, scanning or other - except for brief quotations in critical reviews or articles, without prior written permission of the publisher.

ISBN10 0-615-34744-4

ISBN13 9780615347448

All scripture quotations, unless otherwise indicated, are taken from the HOLY BIBLE, NEW INTERNATIONAL VERSION (NIV) Copyright © 1973, 1978, 1984 by International Bible Society. Used by permission of Zondervan. All rights reserved.

Scripture quotations marked NAU are taken from the New American Updated Version of the Holy Bible.

Cover design and interior layout by Joseph L. Schlosser Jr.
Photo Credits: Fotolia.com
Man photo: © Justinkendra
Woman photo: © BillionPhotos.com
Group photo: © highwaystarz

www.DennyFinnegan.com
www.GoAheadLaunch.com

DEDICATION

First, I give thanks to the Lord for His persistent pursuit of me, and His patient training of me in the work of prayer through the many experiences of my walk with Him. He taught me about prayer and intercession even before I knew the words and definitions to describe it.

Secondly, to my wife Marcia and the many friends who helped me refine the teaching presentation: included are Lance and Jan Borden, John and Lori Stark, Gay Bland, Bob and Pam King, Anne Early and Mary Ellen Connors, as well as, a host of students who allowed me to teach them the material as "test students."

TABLE OF CONTENTS

Forward By Rev. Denny A. Finnegan

Understanding Prayer Ministry   11
    13 Week Small Group Bible Study
    The Purpose Of This Study
    Outline for Understanding Prayer Ministry

Introduction to Prayer   13
    LESSON 1: Two-Way Communication with God
        How Do We Draw Closer To God?   13
        Responding To Jesus When He Calls Us Friend!   14
        A Personal Experiment   15

Section 1: Intercessory Prayer   17
    LESSON 2: Intercessory Prayer
        Three Different Ways We Can Intercede   18
        Discussion   18
        An Intercessory Prayer Model   19
        Application   19
        Let's Pray ...   20
    LESSON 3: Personal Intercession   **21**
        Why We Can Intercede   21
        How Can We Intercede?   23
        A Personal Experiment   25
    LESSON 4: Event Intercession   **27**
        Basic Principles Of Event Intercession   27
        An Example Of Event Intercession   29
        A Personal Experiment   31
    LESSON 5: Strategic Intercession   **33**
        How God Equips and Empowers Us In   33
            Strategic Intercession
        An Example Of Strategic Intercession   35
        A Personal Experiment   36

Section 2: Prophetic Prayer
    LESSON 6: Defining Prophetic Prayer   37
        What's All The Commotion About The Prophetic?   37
        Discussion   37
        One Way To Understand The Prophetic   38

Section 2: Prophetic Prayer (continued)

Discussion	38
So, "How Do You Know If It Is The Holy Spirit Or Not?	38
So, "What Is Prophetic Prayer?"	39
Small Group Prayer Excercise	40

LESSON 7: Prophetic Ministry — 41
- The Gift Of Love — 41
- Gifts Of Prophecy And Tongues — 43
- Small Group Prayer Excercise — 45

LESSON 8: Prophetic Gifts — 47
- The Different Prophetic Gifts — 47
- Discerning The Holy Spirit's Work — 49
- Small Group Prayer Excercise — 50

LESSON 9: Ministering Prophetically — 51
- To The Church In Laodicea — 51
- To The Church In Philadelphia — 52
- To The Church In Ephesus — 53
- Small Group Prayer Excercise — 54

Section 3: Healing Prayer

LESSON 10: Healing Prayer — 55
- Let's Reflect On The Concept Of "God's Salvation" — 55
- Let's Reflect On The Concept Of "God's Peace" — 56
- How Jesus Fulfilled God's Salvation And Peace — 56
- Small Group Discussion — 58

LESSON 11: Inner Healing — 59
- A Definition Of Inner Healing — 59
- Jesus Heals A Paralytic — 60
- Jesus Heals A Sick Woman — 61
- Jesus Heals Through Forgiveness — 61
- Small Group Discussion — 62
- Small Group Prayer Excercise — 63

LESSON 12: Physical Healing — 65
- Reasons Jesus Healed And Why We Should Pray For Healing — 65
- Small Group Discussion — 67
- Small Group Prayer Excercise — 68

LESSON 13: Freedom In Christ — 69
- How Do Christians Join With Jesus In Praying For Freedom In Christ? — 70
- Small Group Discussion — 71
- Small Group Prayer Excercise — 72
- Prayer Journal — 73

FOUNDATIONS - Understanding Prayer Ministry

FORWARD
by Rev. Denny A. Finnegan

Understanding The Need

I have been involved in full-time pastoral ministry since 1983. During this time period, I have been taught and have experienced much about the work of prayer. Even before I entered into ministry, and not long after I came into a personal relationship with Jesus Christ in 1971, I felt both a longing and a need to be engaged in the work of prayer.

This study material is some of the more recent fruit of my walk with Jesus Christ and His call upon my life. It comes from some truths I have witnessed come alive to me through the Scriptures and through my own personal walk with Him; some simple truths that I believe God offers - and calls - all followers of Jesus to have come alive in their own personal walk with Jesus.

Four Simple Truths

TRUTH #1: I call prayer work, not because I see prayer as a spiritual or religious activity by which I am trying to earn anything from God, but because I believe prayer is supposed to be a lifestyle for all believers. And, it takes work - a discipline of focused daily activity to make prayer a consistent and important part of my life. The word discipline is connected to the word disciple.

TRUTH #2: As a pastor, I believe in two important keys to helping the followers of Christ become disciples of Christ. The first key is - to help each follower of Jesus accept personal responsibility for their intimacy with Jesus. The work of prayer begins with the work of relationship with Jesus Christ. And I have seen how prayer has become the language of love and relationship between me and Jesus

TRUTH #3: The second key flows from the first key - as each follower of Jesus accepts personal responsibility for their intimacy with Jesus, they start to take responsibility for their service to Christ.

Two quotes from Scripture, one from the Gospel of John, one from the Book of Hebrews:

I tell you the truth, the Son can do nothing by himself; he can do only what he sees his Father doing, because whatever the Father does the Son also does. 20 For the Father loves the Son and shows him all he does. Yes, to your amazement he will show him even greater things than these. (John 5:19-20 NIV)

It is the Father's desire to show us His will out of His love for each one of us, just as the Father did for His Only Begotten.

Next ...

Let us fix our eyes on Jesus, the author and perfecter of our faith, who for the joy set before Him endured the cross, scorning its shame, and sat down at the right hand of the throne of God. (Hebrews 12:2 NIV)

Out of that place of intimacy with God comes both our discovery of God's will and joy for our lives. God means for our service to Him to spring forth from the love and joy that is sown in our lives, a joy that is boundless and capable of enduring all things for the Lord.

TRUTH #4: While not everyone is called to Intercessory Prayer Ministry, all believers are called to intercede (Ephesians 6:18 NIV). While not everyone is called to Prophetic Prayer Ministry, all believers may pray prophetically (1 Corinthians 14:5 NIV). While not everyone is called to Healing Prayer Ministry, all believers can pray for healing (John 14:12 NIV).

My desire is for the Body of Christ to come alive in the love and grace of Jesus Christ, and to become conduits of Jesus' Life and Light that flow from the throne of God. (Revelation 22:1-5 NIV).

Sincerely Yours in Christ,
Rev. Denny Finnegan

Understanding Prayer Ministry

13 Week Small Group Bible Study

As we begin this study together, there are three "truths" about God's communication with us I have been learning - and relearning - that are important for us to consider before we begin this study together. They are:

1) God's ability to communicate with us will always be greater than our inability to hear - God is not limited by our ability when God wants to communicate with us.

2) God's desire to communicate with us will always be stronger than whatever we may believe about God at any given moment - God is not deterred by our lack of desire when God wants to relate to us.

3) God's delight to communicate with us will always be 'immeasurably more than all we ask or imagine, according to His power that is at work within us' (Ephesians 3:20) - God is not disappointed in us, because God chose us to be His children.

The Purpose Of This Study

The purpose of this study is to provide the opportunity for a "general training and equipping" in the Ministry of Prayer. Our hope for you is three-fold:

1. *To lay a foundation which will help us pray, together as well as privately, with effectiveness and power;*

2. *To encourage those who are already praying that "your prayers do make a difference";*

3. *To help each of us identify what "next steps" we might take in serving the Lord specifically through prayer.*

www.DennyFinnegan.com

Introduction To Prayer

LESSON 1 : TWO-WAY COMMUNICATION WITH GOD

"Come near to God and He will come near to you." (James 4:8)

Those are exciting words from the Apostle James! God wants to draw us close to Him purely because He loves us! He has given us prayer as a *"tool of relationship"* which will help to draw us closer to Him and Him to us. To receive the closeness He offers, we need to understand how to use this gift He has given us.

How Do We Draw Closer To God?

James' instruction is also a promise and there are so many passages in the Bible that demonstrate it. Let's look at one of the songs of prayer written by David, whom the Bible calls *"a man after God's own heart."* David's songs were used for both private and congregational prayer, and they illustrate a wonderful range of ways people may seek God. They also illustrate how God responds to help them find Him.

In Psalm 63, we find a man who will be King running for his life in the Judean desert from the man who is King. It is in adversity that a person's heart is seen most clearly, so in this Psalm we see how David's heart sought God's heart in a very difficult time. Let's focus on Psalm 63:1, one phrase at a time.

In each phrase, describe and discuss:

    a) How each phrase might reflect David's circumstances and feelings;
    b) What it says about David's heart for God (that is, his attitude toward God);
    c) What David seems to understand about God's heart for him.

"O God, You are my God":

"earnestly I seek You": (this phrase could also translate, "early I seek You")

"my soul thirsts for You": (also translates, "my life/appetite is parched for You")

"my body longs for You": (also translates, "my flesh faints for You")

www.DennyFinnegan.com

"in a dry and weary land where there is no water": (also translates, "in a land parched and faint/exhausted worn out of water")

Talk about how David's attitude drew him closer to God; how it might help you draw closer to God.

Responding To Jesus When He Calls Us Friend!

Read John 15:12-17.

What kind of *"friendship"* is God, the Father, offering us through Jesus, the Son?

_____
_____
_____
_____

What does Jesus tell us about friendship? How did He prove this teaching?

_____
_____
_____
_____

What does this teach us about how Jesus relates to us? And how we can relate to Jesus?

_____
_____
_____
_____

Look closely at verse 14: Do you have any friends who might say something like this to you? What would you think if they did? What makes it different for Jesus to ask this of us, and how could our response to this command draw us closer to Christ?

_____
_____
_____
_____

Look closely at verse 15: What do you see there about our relationship with Him?

_____
_____
_____

What parts of this passage are hard to take, and what parts are comforting? What in it do you find particulary helpful?

_____
_____
_____

Now let's look at Jeremiah 29:12-13. How are these verses consistent with what Jesus says?

_____
_____
_____

A Personal Experiment

1. This coming week, read Psalm 63:1-5 every day, Monday through Friday, and read it to God, making David's prayer your prayer too. After you pray it through, spend about one-half hour thinking about these verses, one at a time - or about 5-6 minutes on each verse. You might think about what particular words mean, or you might remember circumstances in your own life when a verse would have been helpful; maybe even a hope or dream that awakens in you. Ask God to help you in your thinking.

This kind of reflection in Scripture is called "meditational prayer" (look at Psalm 1:2). You might even fiind yourself spending the whole time on one verse! Some days you will find it easier to think than other days, so give it a fresh try each day.

2. If you are struggling with what to pray, God has promised to help us. Read Romans 8:26-27. Then ask the Holy Spirit to help you pray wher you feel weak and to help you pray what you ought.

3. Get a notebook and write down your reflections. Write down just what you think, and don't worry about how it looks or sounds. This is an excellent way to keep track of where God may be communicationg to you - where you are also practicing "listening" to God. **Know this truth :** God's ability to speak will ALWAYS be greater than our inability to hear! God wants to communicate with each of us; give Jesus the chance.

4. Write down anything specific you believe God guided you to pray for yourself or for someone else.

The attitude is "flexibility;" the goal is "intimacy with God;" the purpose is "practicing two-way communication and flexibility with God."

Section 1: Intercessory Prayer

LESSON 2 : INTERCESSORY PRAYER

What is Intercessory Prayer? The word "to intercede" means to "intervene between parties with a view to reconciling differences; mediate" (Webster's New Collegiate Dictionary). When we do "intercessory prayer" we are choosing to speak on behalf of someone else to God, the Father, in the Name of Jesus, the Son, just as Jesus, the Son, speaks to the Father on our behalf.

As the writer of Hebrews 4:14-16 says:

"14 Since then we have a great high priest who has passed through the heavens, Jesus the Son of God, let us hold fast our confession. 15 For we do not have a high priest who cannot sympathize with our weaknesses, but One who has been tempted in all things as we are, yet without sin. 16 Let us therefore draw near with confidence to the throne of grace, that we may receive mercy and may find grace to help in time of need." (Hebrews 4:14-16)

Discussion:

1) How does Jesus intercede for us?

_____
_____
_____
_____
_____
_____
_____
_____
_____
_____

2) How can Jesus' work as our "high priest who [can] sympathize with our weaknesses" encourage us to pray for our own needs? for the needs of others?

_____
_____
_____
_____
_____
_____
_____
_____
_____
_____

Three Different Ways We Can Intercede

Because of Jesus, we can now approach God's throne of mercy and grace boldly - for ourselves and for others. When we intercede for someone else, we are choosing to serve them with our prayers, our requests for God's mercy and grace to be poured out upon them.

There are three particular ways that we might find ourselves acting on behalf of someone else with our prayer requests:

Personal Intercession: Praying alone, making petitions for ourselves or for someone else. We could be praying for one person or many people.

Event Intercession: Praying with one person, more than one person or many others, in a particular location. We could be praying for one person or many people.

Strategic Intercession: Praying with one person, more than one person or many others, in a particular location, *with a particular awareness and sense of authority from the Lord to overcome any opposition set up against those for whom we pray.* We could be praying for one person or many people.

Discussion

1) Where have you seen these three different types of intercession take place?

_____
_____
_____
_____

2) Have you ever participated in any of these three different types of intercession? If yes, give details?

_____
_____
_____
_____

3) What are some of your struggles about intercessory prayer? Or any of these three different types of intercession?

_____
_____
_____
_____

An Intercessory Prayer Model

If I were to try and summarize what *"Intercessory Prayer"* is like - what it is we might ask of God for someone - I would use Jesus' own words in response to one of His own followers who said, *"Lord, teach us to pray ..."* (Luke 11:1). In Matthew 6:9-13, Matthew records the more expanded version of Jesus' prayer in Luke 11. The key verse for me is Matthew 6:10, where Jesus teaches us to pray, *"Your kingdom come, Your will be done on earth as it is in heaven."* The phrase, *"Your will be done..."* could also be translated as, *"Your will be birthed..."*. And the verses that follow show specific ways that we are asking for God's will *"to be birthed"* in our lives, in the lives of others, and in our world.

God wants to use our prayers on behalf of others *"to birth His will"*, whether it is through Personal Intercession, Event Intercession, or Strategic Intercession. The next three lessons will give you a general overview of how the Holy Spirit may call you and equip you to serve others with the mercy and grace of God found only in Jesus Christ through prayer.

If you have a desire to see things change in our world or in the lives of others, then you are already called by God to intercede. Let these next 3 lessons further equip you in Intercessory Prayer. But let's end this lesson by breaking into groups of three or four and practice praying the Intercessory Prayer Model Jesus gave to us, His followers.

Application

1) Take each of the following phrases from the *"Our Father"*, and ask God to show you how to pray it, and who to pray it for. It might be for yourself, someone else in your group, or someone outside of your group.

2) Keep your prayers short so that it gives everyone who wants to pray out loud the opportunity to do so.

3) When someone else prays, you have the opportunity to pray in agreement with them, simply by saying, *"Yes, Lord... I agree with that."*

4) You do not have to finish the whole prayer. You have permission to stay with any verse as long as you want.

Let's Pray ...

Vs.9: *"Our Father in heaven, hallowed be Your Name,"* - Spend time thanking God, the Father, for who He is, and for what He has done.

Vs.10: *"Your kingdom come, Your will be done on earth as it is in heaven."* - Spend time asking God, the Father, what it is He wants to do and how He wants to do it: in your life, your church, elsewhere;

Vs.11: *"Give us this day our daily bread."* - Spend time asking God, the Father, with confidence, for your needs, the needs of your church, the needs of others. Then give thanks for what He has already provided!

Vs.12: *"Forgive us our debts, as we also have forgiven our debtors."* - Spend time asking, God, the Father, how you are indebted to Him or to someone else by how you have sinned, (The word, "debt" implies how you have taken away from someone's honor; the word forgive means literally to let go of);

Then ask the Lord to help you let go of your sin. Ask the Lord to help you let go of those who have sinned against you, and have taken some of your honor away.

Vs.13: *"And do not lead us into temptation, but deliver us from evil."* - Close with asking God for His protection for you, for your family, for our church, for others. Then thank and praise Him for His goodness and grace.

LESSON 3 : PERSONAL INTERCESSION

What do we need to know about Personal Intercession?

"Personal Intercession" is where we usually are praying by ourselves in a particular location for ourselves or for someone else. We might be praying for one person or many people. You could be part of a prayer chain, or simply someone who enjoys receiving the prayer requests of other. You could be someone who has a burden to see God change your own family members, specific lives and places in your community, or around the world.

Let's cover some basics for why we can intercede (to act on someone else's behalf through prayer); and how we can intercede (what we could or should ask of God on someone else's behalf).

Why We Can Intercede

"14 Since then we have a great high priest who has passed through the heavens, Jesus the Son of God, let us hold fast our confession. 15 For we do not have a high priest who cannot sympathize with our weaknesses, but One who has been tempted in all things as we are, yet without sin. 16 Let us therefore draw near with confidence to the throne of grace, that we may receive mercy and may find grace to help in time of need." (Hebrews 4:14-16)

1. Hebrews 4:14: There are two specific titles that are given to Jesus in this verse that describe how Jesus intercedes for us - "acts on our behalf": "a great high priest" and "Jesus the Son of God."

How should Jesus acting on our behalf as our "great high priest" increase our confidence to pray?
___
___
___
___

How should Jesus acting on our behalf as "the Son of God" increase our confidence to pray?
___
___
___
___

www.DennyFinnegan.com

The word "confess" means, "to make known", and can also include "positive statements," including "praise." What should we confess about Jesus in our prayers? Why is this important?

_____
_____
_____
_____

2. Hebrews 4:15: This verse describes some of the reasons why Jesus makes such "a great high priest" on our behalf. Looking at these three phrases, let's describe and discuss what they mean for us and our intercessory prayers.

"we do not have a high priest who cannot sympathize with our weaknesses"

"One who has been tempted in all things as we are"

"yet without sin"

3. Hebrews 4:16: This verse gives 3 important truths about Intercessory Prayer: 1) how we should approach; 2) where we should approach; and 3) why we should approach.

How we should approach: *"Let us therefore draw near with confidence ..."*

What does this mean and what might it look like when we pray for ourselves or someone else?

_____
_____
_____

Where we should approach: *"... to the throne of grace ..."*

How should this truth affect our confidence to draw near when we pray for ourselves or for someone else?

_____
_____
_____

Why we should approach: *"that we may receive mercy and may find grace to help in time of need."*

What is it that God offers to give when we pray for ourselves or for someone else? How should this affect our intercessory prayers?

_____
_____
_____
_____

How Can We Intercede?

In this section, we will take a look at how Jesus taught us to pray for ourselves and for others, no matter what type of intercessory prayer we find ourselves burdened or called to do. In this prayer, Jesus taught us how to *"draw near with confidence to the throne of grace, that we may receive mercy and may find grace to help in time of need."* (Hebrews 4:16, NAU)

1. Matthew 6:9: *"Our Father in heaven, hallowed be Your name."*
Why is it good to begin all our intercessory prayers in this way?

_____
_____
_____
_____

2. Matthew 6:10: *"Your kingdom come, Your will be done on earth as it is in heaven."*
If you are not sure what God's will is for a situation, it is good to begin with spending time seeking His will for someone.

What are some of the ways God revealed His will to people in the Bible?

_____
_____
_____
_____

How does God guide you?

_____
_____
_____
_____

3. **Matthew 6:11:** *"Give us today our daily bread."* This is about praying for practical needs.

What are some of the many practical needs you need for the day that someone else might need?

_____
_____
_____
_____

Why should you have confidence that God even cares about these needs?

_____
_____
_____
_____

4. **Matthew 6:12:** *"Forgive us our debts, as we also have forgiven our debtors."*

The word "forgive" means "to let go of." In other words, we are asking for God's power so help someone let go of sin that they have either committed or had committed against them.

How might this kind of prayer be powerful in growing the Kingdom of God? In growing someone's relationship with God?

_____
_____
_____
_____

5. Matthew 6:13: *"And lead us not into temptation, but deliver us from the evil one."*

This verse connects to, *"For we do not have a high priest who cannot sympathize with our weaknesses, but One who has been tempted in all things as we are, yet without sin."* (Hebrews 4:15)

In light of what Jesus has done for us and continue to do for us, how can we pray this prayer with confidence for ourselves? For others?

_____
_____
_____
_____

A Personal Experiment

1. This coming week, spend at least ½ hour each day, Monday through Friday in which you practice praying through the Lord's prayer in **Matthew 6:9-13** for a different person, or group of people, each day.

2. If you are struggling with what to pray, God has promised to help us. **Read Romans 8:26-27**. Then ask the Holy Spirit to help you pray where you feel weak and to help you pray what you ought.

3. Get a notebook and write down your reflections. Write down just what you think, and don't worry about how it looks or sounds. This is an excellent way to keep track of where God may be communicating with you - where you are also practicing "listening" to God.

Know this truth: God's ability to speak will ALWAYS be greater than our inability to hear! God wants to communicate with each of us, give Jesus the chance.

Notes:
_____
_____
_____
_____
_____
_____
_____
_____
_____
_____
_____
_____
_____
_____
_____
_____
_____
_____
_____
_____

LESSON 4 : EVENT INTERCESSION

How do we join our prayers with others in Event Intercession?

"Event Intercession" is very similar to "Personal Intercession" in that you are focused upon *"approaching the throne of grace to find mercy and grace in [the] time of need"* for specific people whom you may or may not know. The biggest difference is that you are intentionally focusing on an event. You could do this as part of a group of intercessors, or by praying on your own before, during and/or after the event.

In this lesson we will look at two particular passages of Scripture: 1) Matthew 18:18-20, some basic principles of corporate event intercession; and 2) Acts 12:1-18, an example of corporate event intercession.

Basic Principles Of Event Intercession

Matthew 18:18-20

This passage is framed by Jesus in the context of someone who sins against you and how the Body of Christ should act in matters of church discipline. But it also concludes with important principles of how we should ask for the Father's *"will be done for you"* when *"two or three come together in [Jesus'] name."* In the Gospel of John, Jesus also instructs us "ask anything of the Father in His name" (John 14:12-14).

I believe that Jesus is also calling us to submit all actions of church discipline to the work of prayer by at least two or three who have come together in [Jesus'] name. Let's take a closer look at some of these principles of corporate prayer.

Matthew 18:18: The Authority We Exercise in Event Intercession

"I tell you the truth, whatever you bind on earth will be bound in heaven, and whatever you loose on earth will be loosed in heaven."

The word "bind" translates as, "tie, imprison, compel, forbid, prohibit", and could even be used to describe what you do when you get married (cf.1 Cor.7:17) ... choosing to "tie yourself" to your spouse. The word "loose" translates as untie, release, set free, break, set aside, pull down, break up, allow. The underlying principle is the exercise of spiritual authority.

What might we be "binding"? What might we be "loosing"?

_____
_____
_____
_____

How might we exercise this kind of spiritual authority in prayer? What might the prayers sound like?
_____
_____
_____

Why would Jesus want His church to exercise this kind of spiritual authority? (cf. Matthew 6:10; 10:7)
_____
_____
_____

2. Matthew 18:19-20: *"The Conditions for Our Spiritual Authority"*

The word, "agree" translates as, "be in agreement with, match, fit together (as in cloth)." The phrase "in my name", carries with it the understanding that as you speak in someone's name, you are seeking to fully represent the will of the one whose name you are using.

vs.19: What is the first type of "agreement-seeking" Jesus wants us to have? Why is this so important for church actions? For corporate prayer?
_____
_____
_____

vs.20: What is the second type of "agreement-seeking" Jesus expects us to have? Why is this so important for church actions? For corporate prayer?
_____
_____
_____

Summary:

Discuss and describe what this type of corporate prayer should be like, both in its exercise of spiritual authority and in its "agreement."
_____
_____
_____
_____

An Example Of Event Intercession

Acts 12:1-18

"Peter's Miraculous Escape From Prison"

1. Read Acts 12:1-5: *"Herod persecutes the church."*

Describe the situation...

_____
_____
_____
_____

What is Peter's predicament? What might Peter be feeling at this point in time?

_____
_____
_____
_____

Vs.5: *"The church was earnestly praying to God for him."* In other words, the early church started to do Event Intercession on Peter's behalf.

What would be some reasons for their prayers on behalf of Peter? Some of the benefits?

_____
_____
_____
_____

2. Read Acts 12:6-11: *"Peter is Miraculously Set Free from Prison"*

What do you think Peter's prayers may have been like in this situation? (compare with Ephesians 3:20)

_____
_____
_____
_____

What was Peter's role in this "miraculous escape"? How did God expect Peter to cooperate with those who prayed?

_____
_____
_____
_____

www.DennyFinnegan.com

Compare Peter's response in verses 8-10 and vs.11 - the before and after of all these prayers. How are Peter's expectations in prayer and his reaction to answered prayer much like our own?

_____
_____
_____
_____
_____

3. Read Acts 12:12-17: *"The Church's Reaction to Answered Prayer"*

This is a concrete example of "someone bound" being "loosed!" (see Matthew 18:18-20)

What do you think some of their prayers may have been like? (compare with Ephesians 3:20)

_____
_____
_____
_____
_____

How are the church's expectations in prayer and their reaction to answered prayer much like our own?

_____
_____
_____
_____
_____

What are some of the many ways you see God's grace demonstrated in their prayers? (compare with Ephesians 3:20)

_____
_____
_____
_____
_____

What are some of the ways you are encouraged about Event Intercession ?

_____
_____
_____
_____
_____

A Personal Experiment

1. This coming week, find or form a group of people with whom to pray. It can be as few as two or three others. Practice listening to the Lord in order to be in agreement with Him; then practice praying in agreement with each other.

If you sense permission from the Lord to "exercise authority", then "bind and loose" as the Holy Spirit leads you; if you do not sense this type of permission, you can still plead on their behalf.

Remember Ephesians 3:20 as you pray...

2. If you are struggling with what to pray, God has promised to help us. Read Romans 8:26-27. Then ask the Holy Spirit to help you pray where you feel weak and to help you pray what you ought.

3. Get a notebook and write down your reflections. Write down just what you think, and don't worry about how it looks or sounds. This is an excellent way to keep track of where God may be communicating with you - where you are also practicing "listening" to God.

Know this truth: God's ability to speak will ALWAYS be greater than our inability to hear! God wants to communicate with each of us, give Jesus the chance.

Notes:

LESSON 5 : STRATEGIC INTERCESSION

What do we need to know about Strategic Intercession?

Our lesson on "Strategic Intercession" comes last in this section on Intercessory prayer, because it builds upon components, principles and faith-experiences in the other two styles of intercession - learning how to intercede personally for others (Personal Intercession); and learning how to cooperate wth the Holy Spirit and with others in intercessory prayer (Event Intercession).

A child of God may engage in "Strategic Intercession" in his or her own "Personal Intercession" times, as led by the Holy Spirit, and when cooperating in prayer with others for specific events or activities. A group of intercessiors may sense a specific call from the Lord to enter into a strategic time of prayer due to a strategic work for the advance of God's Kingdom that is about to take place.

To better understand this type of Intercessory Prayer, we are goiing to examine two passages of Scripture: 1) Ephesians 6:10-20, where the Apostle Paul describes how Jesus equips and empowers us for strategic intercession. God may call us to do this type of intercession so that our prayers will work to advance God's promises and plans for His people, and 2) Joshua 5:13- 6:7 where Joshua leads the people of Israel into both a literal and spiritual battle against the city of Jericho whose citizens opposed the fulfillment of God's promises and plans for His people.

How God Equips and Empowers Us In Strategic Intercession

Ephesians 6:10-20

1. Read Ephesians 610-13: *"God Desires for Us to Overcome in the Strength of His Mighty Power"*

List all the words in the passage that have to do with "strength and power;" then discuss God's desire for us in the work of advanciing His kingdom.

_____
_____
_____
_____

What examples of God's power at work in and through people can you recall in the Bible? Do you believe that God still works in these ways today?

_____
_____
_____
_____

www.DennyFinnegan.com

According to vs.12, who is our real enemy? Why, then, is God's power necessary for this kind of warfare?

Summarize:

What are the purposes behind God's provision of His Power to us?

2. Read Ephesians 6:14-20: *"God's Multi-faceted Provisions of Power"*

Reminder: Each piece of armor reflects both "the character" and "the work" of God in creation and in our lives!

List each piece of armor Paul mentions. Then discuss: a) How each piece displays God's strength and power; and, b) How each piece strengthens us "in the Lord?"

How does "praying in the Spirit" (vs.18) activate the "strength of God's armor?"

"Praying in the Spirit" is NOT just about the "gift of tongues," but about letting the Holy Spirit guide our prayers. How have you seen the Holy Spirit work in this way in your life?

How does this kind of praying help ministry happen like it did for Paul (cf. vs.19-20)? help advance the Kingdom of God?

An Example Of Strategic Intercession

Joshua 5:13-6:7 "The Fall of Jericho"

1. Read Joshua 5:13-15: *"God Prepares Joshua for Battle"*

In verse 13, Joshua asks this "commander of the army of the Lord" an important question: "Are you for us or for our enemies?" His reply is, "Neither!" I believe God is making an important point here: "Before God is for us, we need to be for God."

There are least three ways Joshua prepares spiritually for the physical battle that is about to take place. What are they? (Clue: two are in verse 14; one is in verse 15).

_____
_____
_____
_____

What does that mean for us? How should we prepare for "spiritual battle" when we sense God's call?

_____
_____
_____
_____

2. Read Joshua 6:1-7: *"Joshua Receives God's Battle Plans"*

How did Joshua's preparation prepare him to receive God's strategies for battle? Prepare him to act?

_____
_____
_____
_____

Describe God's battle plan. It was all lead by worship leaders and by the Ark of the Covenant, which represented the Presence of God. What is the symbolism in its design?

_____
_____
_____
_____

Each piece of armor in Ephesians 6:14-18 represents some aspect of God's character they needed to win this battle and claim God's promises for them.

Discuss how each *"piece of armor"* is needed to strengthen them for this unique kind of warfare.
_____
_____
_____
_____

How was their obedience to the plan like praying in the Spirit? ... like an act of worship?
_____
_____
_____
_____

(Note: This is a good example of what "prayer walking" is like - a specific way God may lead people to "act-out" Strategic Intercession.)

A Personal Experiment

1. This coming week, find or form a group of people to pray with. It can be as few as two or three others. Read Matthew 18:18-20 together. Practice listening to the Lord in order to be in agreement with Him; then practice praying in agreement with each other.

If you sense permission from the Lord to *"exercise authority,"* then *"bind and loose"* as the Holy Spirit leads you; if you do not sense this type of permission, you can still plead on their behalf. Remember Ephesians 3:20 as you pray.

2. If you are struggling with what to pray, God has promised to help us. Read Romans 8:26-27. Then ask the Holy Spirit to help you pray where you feel weak and to help you pray what you ought.

3. Get a notebook and write down your reflections. Write down just what you think, and don't worry about how it looks or sounds. This is an excellent way to keep track of where God may be communicating with you - where you are also practicing "listening" to God.

Know this truth: God's ability to speak will ALWAYS be greater than our inability to hear! God wants to communicate with each of us, give Jesus the chance.

Section 2: Prophetic Prayer

LESSON 6 : DEFINING PROPHETIC PRAYER

What's All The Commotion About The Prophetic?

The word "prophetic" causes quite a stir in many churches. The reactions range from skepticism to conviction, fear to joy. This wide range of reactions stem from the many views about "the prophetic" and "prophetic gifts" that exist within the various "streams of faith;" 1) some believe that all prophetic gifts have ceased and are no longer relevant to the Body of Christ, because "the perfect" has come in the completion of revelation with the canon of Scripture; 2) some believe that some prophetic gifts are still present, but rarely manifested in the Body of Christ today; and 3) others believe that all prophetic gifts still continue to be relevant to the Body of Christ today, as long as what is revealed is in agreement with the Word of God and submitted to those in spiritual authority over the individuals exercising prophetic gifts.

Discussion:

1) What would you say best describes your views about the prophetic?
___
___
___
___
___
___
___

2) What scares you about the prophetic?
___
___
___
___
___
___
___

3) Have you ever had a good experience with the prophetic? If you wish, please briefly share?
___
___
___
___
___
___
___

www.DennyFinnegan.com

One Way To Understand The Prophetic

The Holy Spirit reveals through the Apostle John, in the last part of Revelation 19:10, *"For the testimony of Jesus is the spirit of prophecy."* That gives us a few truths about prophecy in the New Testament:

1) Prophecy should always point back to Jesus.

2) Prophecy is grounded in either what Jesus has done for us or what Jesus wants to do for us.

We can be prophetic simply by sharing what Jesus has done for us, either through the reading of Scripture, or from in our own personal lives.

In other the words, the last time you shared a scripture verse with someone to encourage, comfort or strengthen them, if you believe God guided you to share it, you were probably being prophetic. And, if you ever shared with someone how God was at work in your life, and it encouraged, comforted or strengthened them, then the Holy Spirit was working through you prophetically!

Discussion

1) Can you think of a time someone shared a scripture verse or a personal experience with you that encouraged, comforted or strengthened you in your relationship with Jesus? Please share briefly, if you feel comfortable doing so.

_____
_____
_____
_____

Can you think of a time God used you to share a scripture verse or personal experience with someone else that encouraged, comforted or strengthened them in their relationship with Jesus? Please briefly share, if you feel comfortable doing so.

_____
_____
_____
_____

So, "How Do You Know If It Is The Holy Spirit Or Not?"

There are at least four Biblical tests we can use to discern if the Holy Spirit is at work. Let's discuss each of these:

1) Does it give glory to Jesus Christ in the present and in the future? Look up these verses and discuss them: John 14:26; 16:13-14.

2) Is it consistent with the intentions and character of God as revealed in Scripture? Look up these verses and discuss them: John 2:22; 2 Timothy 3:14-17.

3) Do other people who are sensitive to Jesus' leading confirm what is being said or being done? Look up these verses and discuss them: Acts 15:28; 1 Corinthians 14:29.

4) Is there confirmation through events or the facts? (Sometimes we have to wait and see if the events that happen afterwards confirm or prove that this is the Holy Spirit; sometimes we have to cooperate with the Holy Spirit by praying about the results.) Look up these verses and discuss them: Deuteronomy 18:21-22; Isaiah 55:10-11; 1 John 4:1.

So, "What Is Prophetic Prayer?"

One way to begin answering this question is to begin by asking some questions: *"Have you ever wondered about God's will for your life? Have you ever asked God for the wisdom to know what to do? Or even how to counsel someone else in a difficult situation?"* These questions assume that there is a God who wants to communicate with us and can communicate with us... and God DOES want to communicate with us! When you ask questions like these, you are hoping - maybe even expecting - God to answer them. That means you are seeking "prophetic guidance" from God, in accordance with the Word of God, that is discerned as a result of either your prayers or the prayers of others. As the Apostle Paul states about "the prophetic" in 1 Corinthians 14:3, *"But everyone who prophesies speaks to men for their strengthening, encouragement and comfort."* God wants to guide us in His will for our lives and in His will for His Kingdom.

And, in "Prophetic Prayer," we are trusting that both God's ability and desire to communicate His will to us is greater than our inability (and sometimes even our desire to know) what God's will is for our lives.

Prophetic Prayer does not have to be something scary or unbelievable if we are submitted both to the Word of God and to those in spiritual authority over us. When we are submitted to the Holy Spirit's guidance in both what we say and how we say it - always surrendered to the love of God in Jesus Christ - it can be a powerful tool of ministry to others.

The next three lessons will seek to introduce us to "Prophetic Prayer Ministry" by asking three questions, one for each of the next three lessons:

Lesson 7: What Does the Bible Teach About Prophetic Ministry?

Lesson 8: What Does the Bible Teach About Prophetic Gifts?

Lesson 9: How Can We Minister Prophetically?

But let's end this lesson time by breaking into small groups and practice listening to the Holy Spirit in our prayers for each other.

Small Group Prayer Excercise

1) Have one person in the group volunteer to receive prayer.

2) Let each person in the group quiet his or her heart before the Lord. Tell Jesus you are willing to let the Holy Spirit guide you.

3) Then ask in faith if the Lord has a Scripture verse, or some word that He would have you share for the person who volunteered to receive prayer that might encourage, comfort or strengthen them.

4) Before you pray the Scripture verse or word, in faith, share it with them. Then if they confirm that it "seems to be from the Lord", turn it into a prayer.

5) If you do not get any particular sense of guidance at this time, that's all right... that happens to us all!

6) After awhile, if there is time, you can ask for another volunteer.

LESSON 7 : PROPHETIC MINISTRY

What does the Bible say about Prophetic Ministry?

The Apostle Paul spends a great deal of time talking about the Prophetic in 1 Corinthians 14:1-40, with also some very important foundational teaching about how all ministry is to be done in 1 Corinthians 13:1-13.

These will be the two main sections of our Bible Study: 1). "The Gift of Love", 1 Corinthians 13:1-13; and, 2) Gifts of Prophecy and Tongues, 1 Corinthians 14:1-40.

The Gift Of Love

1 Corinthians 13:1-13

1. **Vs.1-3:** *Pursuing the Gift or the Giver.*

List the different gifts mentioned in these verses.

_____
_____
_____
_____

How is the effect of each gift described when God's love is absent?

_____
_____
_____
_____

The Love of God is essential to the exercise and use of these spiritual gifts. Why? Are any spiritual gifts to be absent from the Love of God?

_____
_____
_____
_____

2. **Vs.4-7:** *The Qualities of God's Love.*

List all the qualities of God's love.

_____
_____
_____
_____

How is God's love to transform us? To transform our use of spiritual gifts?

___

3. Vs.8-12: *"When perfection comes ..."*

Some churches teach that *"when perfection comes"* (vs.10) refers to when the Bible, in its current form, was finalized. Therefore "revelation gifts"- such as tongues, prophecy, and knowledge - have ceased, because *"when perfection comes, the imperfect disappears."*

What do you believe about this?

___

Some churches teach that Paul is referring to the time period when Christ returns and establishes His Kingdom here on earth. They refer to Philippians 1:6, where Paul's phrase, *"carry it on to completion"* is the same root Greek word used for perfection in 1 Corinthians 13:10. Therefore, until we *"know fully"* and are *"fully known,"* the "revelation gifts" are still necessary to the ministry of Jesus' church.

Do you believe Christ's *"perfection has come"* to Christ's church? To us individually? Why, or why not?

___

Do you believe these "revelation gifts" are still necessary to the ministry of the church? Why, or why not?

___

4. Vs.13: *"These three remain ..."*

How are these three Christian virtues essential to the Christian life?

___

How are these three Christian virtues essential to the way we minister with spiritual gifts?

___

Any other questions you have about this passage?

Now let's turn our attention to two main gifts associated with the prophetic.

Gifts of Prophecy and Tongues

1 Corinthians 14:1-40

We will not be able to do an exhaustive study on these two gifts, nor on all of the verses. But this passage will help us understand some principles that should guide us in how the prophetic, undergirded and guided by the Love of God in Christ Jesus (cf. 1 Corinthians 14:1), is to be practiced and exercised in the context of the church of Jesus Christ.

1. Read Vs.1-5: *"... I would rather have you prophesy."* (vs.5)

How does Paul describe the differences between the gift of tongues and the gift of prophecy?

_____
_____
_____
_____

In verse 3, Paul talks about God's purposes for prophetic ministry and prophetic prayer. What are they?

_____
_____
_____
_____

In verse 5, Paul says that there are times when speaking in tongues changes to the prophetic. What makes the difference?

_____
_____
_____
_____

2. Read Vs. 13-17: *"... pray that he may interpret what he says."* [vs.13 (Paul sums up vs.6-12 in vs.13-17)]

Paul distinguishes between "a message in tongues" that is personal and "a message in tongues" that is for the Body of Christ (cf. vs.17).

What is the difference in the two purposes? Are both important to the Lord? Why or why not?

_____
_____
_____
_____

3. Vs.18-25: *"God is really among you!"* (vs.25)

In verses 22, Paul says that, *"Tongues are a sign ... for unbelievers."* The Greek word for "sign" could also be translated as "mark, signal, indication." It "marks" that something "spiritual" is happening. But it is not something with which people who do not have this gift can readily "connect to God," because the message is "unintelligible" to them (cf. vs.19) - unless it is accompanied by the spiritual gift - interpretation of tongues.

In the context of general worship, as opposed to personal prayer in worship, the purpose of both prophecy and interpreted-tongues is "two-fold": a) to instruct (vs.19); and b) to convince (vs.24-25).

In verses 24-25, Paul summarizes the benefits of "prophecy" and "interpreted tongues". List them ...

_____
_____
_____

How will these results give glory to God and increase worship of God?

_____
_____
_____

4. Vs.26-33: *"The spirits of prophets are subject to the control of prophets."* (vs.32)

In verses 26-28, Paul gives guidelines for how the gift of tongues is to be exercised during worship.

What are the guidelines?

_____
_____

In verse 28, Paul distinguishes between "keep quiet in the church" and "speak to himself and God". What are these differences?

_____
_____

In verses 29-33, Paul gives guidelines for how the gift of prophecy is to be exercised during worship.

What are the guidelines?

_____
_____
_____

What does Paul mean when he says, "The spirits of prophets are subject to the control of prophets" (vs.32)?

_____
_____
_____

Small Group Prayer Exercise

(Like the previous week)

1) Have one person in the group volunteer to receive prayer.

2) Let each person in the group quiet his or her heart before the Lord. Tell Jesus you are willing to let the Holy Spirit guide you.

3) Then ask in faith if the Lord has a Scripture verse, or some word He would have you share for the person who volunteered to receive prayer that might encourage, comfort or strengthen them.

4) Before you pray the Scripture verse or word, in faith, share it with them. Then if they confirm that it "seems to be from the Lord", turn it into a prayer.

5) If you do not get any particular sense of guidance, that's all right... that happens to us all!

6) After awhile, if there is time, you can ask for another volunteer.

LESSON 8 : PROPHETIC GIFTS

What does the Bible say about Prophetic Gifts?

This lesson will be divided into two parts. In Part 1, we will look at the three different prophetic gifts the Apostle Paul lists in 1 Corinthians 12:8-10 with examples of each from the New Testament. In Part 2, as the Apostle John charges us to do in 1 John 4:1, we will consider "four tests" that we can use to help us discern "what is from the Holy Spirit of God" and "what is not."

The Different Prophetic Gifts

(1 Corinthians 12:8-10)

"8 For to one is given the word of wisdom through the Spirit, and to another the word of knowledge according to the same Spirit; 9 to another faith by the same Spirit, and to another gifts of healing by the one Spirit, 10 and to another the effecting of miracles, and to another prophecy, and to another the distinguishing of spirits..."

In the previous lesson we looked at the gift of prophecy and also how the gift of tongues may be used by the Lord as a form of the gift of "prophecy" when it is accompanied by the gift of "interpretation of tongues." So we will not repeat discussion of these two prophetic gifts. In this lesson, we will focus on the gifts of: 1) "the word of knowledge," 2) "the word of wisdom," and 3) "the distinguishing of spirits." Because of how the gifts "the word of knowledge" and "the word of wisdom" often operate together, I have switched their order of discussion from the order they appear in the text.

"The Word of Knowledge:" a "word of knowledge" gives "information" about people or situations.

An account of Jesus healing a paralytic is in Matthew 9:2-8, Mark 2:2-12 and Luke 5:18-26. This is just one of many instances where Jesus demonstrated this particular 'gift of the Spirit'. For discussion purposes, read the text from Matthew 9:2-4.

How did Jesus demonstrate "the gift of knowledge" with the paralytic? With the teachers of the law?
_____
_____
_____

Why is this spiritual gift important to the Body of Christ?
_____
_____
_____

2) "The Word of Wisdom:" a *"word of wisdom"* gives *"application"* for people or situations.

In this next text, we will see how *"the word of knowledge"* and *"the word of wisdom"* often operate together. This situation is recorded in Matthew 22:15-21, Mark 12:13-17 and Luke 20:20-25. For discussion purposes, read the text from Luke 20:20-25.

How does Jesus demonstrate *"the gift of wisdom"* in this situation?

_____
_____
_____

How do the gifts *"word of knowledge"* and *"word of wisdom"* cooperate?

_____
_____
_____

Why is this spiritual gift important to the Body of Christ?

_____
_____
_____

3) "The Distinguishing of Spirits:" *"distinguishing of spirits"* helps us discern "the motivating influence".

The Bible uses the word "spirit" to include any of the following meanings: "angels, demons, the human spirit, the Holy Spirit, an anointing, mantles, the motivating influence of a person" ("You May All Prophesy", page 12; by Steve Thompson). In many of the passages where Jesus demonstrates "the word of knowledge" and "the word of wisdom", there seems implied that Jesus also discerned the motivating influence of those people involved. But for this part of our study, we will look to the Apostle Paul's experience, as reported by Luke in Acts 16:16-18. Read Acts 16:16-18.

[*Note: The phrase "spirit by which she predicted the future" is also translated as "spirit of divination; or "python spirit" connected to one of the deities (Apollo) and temples in this part of the world (the temple in Delphi).]

What "motivating influence" did Paul discern in this slave girl?

_____
_____
_____
_____

Did she speak the truth? So, why was it important for people to know that this was not the Holy Spirit speaking through her?

_____
_____
_____
_____

FOUNDATIONS - Understanding Prayer Ministry

Why is this spiritual gift important to the Body of Christ?

___

Discerning The Holy Spirit's Work

Four Tests

(Resource adapted from Presbyterian-Reformed Ministries International)

Test #1: "Does the leading or guidance give glory to Jesus Christ?"

"13 But when he, the Spirit of truth, comes, he will guide you into all truth. He will not speak on his own; he will speak only what he hears, and he will tell you what is yet to come. 14 He will bring glory to me by taking from what is mine and making it known to you." (John 16:13-14)

Why is it important to ask this question when discerning guidance from the Lord?

___

Point: The Holy Spirit only glorifies and testifies to Jesus as Lord and God. (See also: John 1:15;15:26; Acts 4:33; 10:43; Romans 3:21; Hebrews 10:15;1 John 5:6)

Test #2: "Is it consistent with the intentions and character of God as revealed in Scripture?"

"After he was raised from the dead, his disciples recalled what he had said. Then they believed the Scripture and the words that Jesus had spoken." (John 2:22)

Why is it important to ask this question when discerning guidance from the Lord?

___

Point: God will not contradict Himself or His truth. (Confer also: John 5:19-20; 32-37; 2 Timothy 3:14-17)

Test #3: "Do other people who are also led by the Holy Spirit have a confirming witness?"

"Two or three prophets should speak, and the others should weigh carefully what is said."
    (1 Corinthians 14:29)

Why is it important to ask this question when discerning guidance from the Lord?

___

www.DennyFinnegan.com

Point: God expects us to exercise our gifts within a context of "accountability" and "mutual submission" within the Body of Christ. Beware of the person who resists being under authority! (See also: Romans 8:6-8; 13:1; 1 Corinthians 14:29-32; 16:15-16; Ephesians 5:21; Hebrews 13:17; James 4:7)

Test #4: "Is there objective confirmation in events or facts?

"10 As the rain and the snow come down from heaven, and do not return to it without watering the earth and making it bud and flourish, so that it yields seed for the sower and bread for the eater, 11 so is my word that goes out from my mouth: It will not return to me empty, but will accomplish what I desire and achieve the purpose for which I sent it." (Isaiah 55:10-11)

Why is it important to ask this question when discerning guidance from the Lord?
_____
_____
_____

Point: The Lord reveals His will for a purpose - "not to return to Me empty". Sometimes, that means we must cooperate with the Holy Spirit through our "prayers" and "perseverance" guided by the word which the Lord sends; sometimes it means waiting for God's timing to come into alignment with preparation God is at work to accomplish within us. (See also: Deuteronomy 18:21-22; Romans 7:4; Galatians 5:22; Ephesians 5:7-10; Colossians 1:6,10; James 3:17)

Small Group Prayer Exercise

(Like the previous week)

1) Have one person in the group volunteer to receive prayer.

2) Let each person in the group quiet his or her heart before the Lord. Tell Jesus you are willing to let the Holy Spirit guide you.

3) Then ask in faith if the Lord has a Scripture verse, or some word He would have you share for the person who volunteered to receive prayer that might encourage, comfort or strengthen them.

4) Before you pray the Scripture verse or word, in faith, share it with them. Then if they confirm that it "seems to be from the Lord", turn it into a prayer.

5) If you do not get any particular sense of guidance, that's all right... that happens to us all!

6) After awhile, if there is time, you can ask for another volunteer.

LESSON 9 : MINISTERING PROPHETICALLY

How can we Minister Prophetically?

In the previous 3 lessons, we have looked at: What Prophetic Prayer Is; What the Bible Teaches About Prophetic Ministry; and What the Bible Teaches About Prophetic Gifts. In this lesson, we will bring these components together and look at 3 different biblical examples of people being ministered to prophetically.

We will be analyzing the prophetic words that Jesus spoke to the Apostle John through the power of the Holy Spirit in the Book of Revelations; more specifically, the three "words" the Lord Jesus revealed to the Church at Laodicea, the Church at Philadelphia, and the Church at Ephesus.

Since the Apostle Paul reveals, in 1 Corinthians 14:3, that the purpose of prophetic ministry is for our *"strengthening, encouragement and comfort,"* we are going to examine how Jesus accomplished this for His people in each of these churches, and look to see how the spiritual gifts of *"word of knowledge," "word of wisdom"* and *"discernment of spirits"* are present in each of these vital prophetic messages.

But before we begin to examine these passages, I want to encourage you NOT to be intimidated or distracted by the type of prophetic experience the Apostle John had in order to receive these prophetic words. We do not have to have the same type of spiritual experience as John (or anyone else) in order for the Holy Spirit to communicate to us from Jesus the same types of revelation, guidance and information that will be useful for someone's *"strengthening, encouragement and comfort."* Remember, there was only one "burning bush" encounter in the whole Bible!

It is not just our spiritual ability that Jesus is looking for, but our spiritual availability that matters to Him. If the Holy Spirit could use Balaam's donkey to deliver a prophetic word, then we should not worry too much about our sense of usefulness to God (Numbers 22:21-35)!

Try to get through all three churches - but you do not have to. Save time for the Small Group Prayer Exercise at the end.

To The Church In Laodicea

Read Revelation 3:14-22.

Notes: Laodicea was known for its production of an eye salve that required very hot water and very cold water. Jesus is not telling them to be for (hot) or against (cold) Him; rather to be useful for Him (since lukewarm water was not useful to them in making this eye salve). They also had become very rich from this product.

In what ways do you see Jesus speaking for their *"strengthening, encouragement and comfort?"*

_____
_____
_____

How do you see each of these spiritual gifts - *"word of knowledge," "word of wisdom"* and *"discernment of spirits"* - present in this prophetic message?

_____
_____
_____

What is upon Jesus' heart for them?

_____
_____
_____

How is this message still relevant to us today?

_____
_____
_____

Has anyone ever ministered to you with similar types of messages?

_____
_____
_____

To The Church In Philadelphia

Read Revelation 3:7-13.

Notes: In the New Testament, the announcement of Jesus' return (*"I am coming soon,"* vs.11) was often used two ways - as a warning to those not paying attention; as a word of exhortation to persevere. Two other phrases to note: 1) vs.7: *"Open doors"* often symbolize *"opportunities to minister"* 2) vs.12: *"Never again will he leave it"* could refer to the frequent earthquakes experienced in this area, and the way people had to *"flee quickly"* and *"return with uncertainty."*

In what ways do you see Jesus speaking for their *"strengthening, encouragement and comfort?"*
_____
_____
_____

How do you see each of these spiritual gifts - *"word of knowledge," "word of wisdom"* and *"discernment of spirits"* - present in this prophetic message?
_____
_____
_____

What is upon Jesus' heart for them?
_____
_____

How is this message still relevant to us today?
_____
_____
_____

Has anyone ever ministered to you with similar types of messages?
_____
_____
_____

To The Church In Ephesus

Read Revelation 2:1-7.

Notes: Vs.1: *"The seven stars"* represent the 7 angels assigned to the churches; and *"the seven lampstands"* appears to refer to the *"witness-light"* that comes from each church (cf. Rev.1:16,20;2:1); vs.6: *"the Nicolaitans"* seems to be closely connected to those spoken of in Pergamum (Rev.2:14-15) and Thyatira (Rev.2:20); the word *"Nicolaitans"* could be connected to two Greek words that mean *"to conquer the people"*, which is similar to the word *"Balaam"* which is connected to the Hebrew word with the same meaning, *"to conquer the people"*. In Pergamum and Thyatira, it was not *"attack from the outside"* but from inside the church they faced - the claims that they were not "destroying Christianity but presenting an improved version" of it (William Barkley, "The Revelation of John", page 66).

In what ways do you see Jesus speaking for their *"strengthening, encouragement and comfort?"*
_____
_____
_____

How do you see each of these spiritual gifts - *"word of knowledge," "word of wisdom"* and *"discernment of spirits"* - present in this prophetic message?
_____
_____
_____

What is upon Jesus' heart for them?
_____
_____
_____

How is this message still relevant to us today?
_____
_____
_____

Has anyone ever ministered to you with similar types of messages?
_____
_____
_____

Small Group Prayer Exercise

(Like the previous week)

1. Have one person in the group volunteer to receive prayer.

2) Let each person in the group quiet his or her heart before the Lord. Tell Jesus you are willing to let the Holy Spirit guide you.

3) Then ask in faith if the Lord has a Scripture verse, or some word He would have you share for the person who volunteered to receive prayer that might encourage, comfort or strengthen them.

4) Before you pray the Scripture verse or word, in faith, share it with them. Then if they confirm that it "seems to be from the Lord," turn it into a prayer.

5) If you do not get any particular sense of guidance, that's all right... that happens to us all!

6) After awhile, if there is time, you can ask for another volunteer.

Section 3: Healing Prayer

LESSON 10 : HEALING PRAYER

What do we mean by Healing Prayer?

There are many theological words used to describe what Jesus accomplished for us on the cross. I am going to mention just two as we start our studies on Healing Prayer. These two words are: "salvation" and "peace". Both of these concepts are solidly grounded in the Old Testament. But they take on a whole new level of benefit for us in light of what Jesus did for us on the cross. As Jesus said in Matthew 5:17, *"Do not think that I have come to abolish the Law or the Prophets; I have not come to abolish them but to fulfill them."*

So we begin our study about Healing Prayer in the Old Testament; because God was healing people even then (e.g., Gen.20:17; Num.12:10,13-15; 21:8-9; Deut.32:39; 1 Sam.6:3; 1 Kings 17:17-24; 2 Kings 5:1ff; 20:5; 2 Chron.7:14; 30:20; Job 42:10-17). It is not just something new with the New Testament! But Healing Prayer does take on a whole new level of accomplishment in the New Testament because of Jesus.

Let's look at the roots of these two words and how Jesus fulfills them in Himself.

Let's Reflect On The Concept Of "God's Salvation"

Psalm 98:1-3 declares that 'the salvation of our God" is connected to all the *"wonderful things"* God has accomplished for His people. The root meaning for the word *"salvation"* is *"to salvage,"* and a dictionary meaning for *"salvage"* is "something saved from destruction or waste so that it can be put to further use," or "the rescue and use of something found or discarded" (The Free Dictionary by Farlex: http://www.thefreedictionary.com/). The Hebrew word for "salvation" is also closely connected to the Hebrew pronunciation of Jesus' Name, *"Yeshua/Joshua,"* which means, *"He saves."*

Share some examples of God acting on behalf of His people *"to save/rescue them from destruction in order to put them to further use"* that you remember from the Old Testament:

_____
_____
_____
_____

How did Jesus' followers continue to demonstrate *"the salvation of our God"*?

_____
_____
_____
_____

www.DennyFinnegan.com

Let's Reflect On The Concept Of "God's Peace"

In Numbers 6:23-27, the Lord commands that His "peace" be a part of the priestly benediction that the priests of God are to pronounce upon all God's people. The Hebrew word for peace, "shalom," is an incredibly rich concept that also included the ideas of "wholeness, completeness, soundness, safety, reward, prosperity, welfare, tranquility, contentment, quiet, friendship."

The Book of Hebrews directly refers to Jesus as our high priest in the New Covenant 14 times; and it is a "priestly work" Jesus also passes onto Jesus' followers. As it is written in 1 Peter 2:5,9, *"But you are a chosen people, a royal priesthood, a holy nation, a people belonging to God, that you may declare the praises of him who called you out of darkness into his wonderful light."*

Share some examples of God acting on behalf of His people to "turn his face toward [them] and give [them] peace" that you remember from the Old Testament:

_____
_____
_____
_____

Share examples from the New Testament where Jesus continued to bless people with "God's Peace:"

_____
_____
_____
_____

How did Jesus' followers continue to bless people with "God's Peace?"

_____
_____
_____
_____

How Jesus Fulfilled God's Salvation and Peace

According to the Gospel of Luke, right after Jesus came back from the wilderness, and after He had overcome the temptations the devil brought against Him (Luke 4:1-13), Jesus returned to Galilee *"in the power of the Spirit,"* and shows up in His home town synagogue in Nazareth on the Sabbath Day (Luke 4:14-30). Jesus read from this text to announce His Great Commission that God, the Father, had given Him as prophesied long ago through the Prophet Isaiah (Isaiah 61:1-2). Here is what Luke records:

17 The scroll of the prophet Isaiah was handed to him. Unrolling it, he found the place where it is written: 18 "The Spirit of the Lord is on me, because he has anointed me to preach good news to the poor. He has sent me to proclaim freedom for the prisoners and recovery of sight for the blind, to release the oppressed, 19 to proclaim the year of the Lord's favor." 20 Then he rolled up the scroll, gave it back to the attendant and sat down. The eyes of everyone in the synagogue were fastened on him, 21 and he began by saying to them, "Today this scripture is fulfilled in your hearing."

"The Spirit of the Lord" came upon Jesus to accomplish and fulfill God's salvation and peace in at least four different ways: 1) *"to preach good news to the poor,"* 2) *"to proclaim freedom for the prisoners,"* 3) *"recovery of sight for the blind,"* and, 4) *"to release the oppressed."*

How might Jesus *"preaching good news to the poor (or pitiful)"* bring God's salvation? Bring God's peace? Bring God's healing?

_____
_____
_____

How might Jesus *"proclaiming freedom (or forgiveness, cancellation of sin) for the prisoners"* bring God's salvation? Bring God's peace? Bring God's healing?

_____
_____
_____

How might Jesus bringing *"recovery/restoration of sight for the blind"* bring God's salvation? Bring God's peace? Bring God's healing?

_____
_____
_____

How might Jesus *"releasing the oppressed (or weakened, broken in pieces, downtrodden)"* bring God's salvation? Bring God's peace? Bring God's healing?

_____
_____
_____

www.DennyFinnegan.com

Small Group Discussion

1) What are some ways you have personally experienced God's salvation at work within your life?

2) What are some ways you have personally experienced God's peace at work within your life?

3) What are some ways you have personally experienced God's healing at work within your life?

4) What are some of the difficulties - or problems - you have about healing prayer?

Close in Prayer for Each Other As the Lord Leads You to Pray ...

LESSON 11 : INNER HEALING

What happens when we pray for Inner Healing?

Nowhere in the Bible does it mention the phrase, "Inner Healing." But then again, it also does not mention the word "Trinity." Yet what we believe about both comes from the observations we have of "God at work" both in the Scriptures and in our world.

It is some of these observations and conclusions about "Inner Healing Prayer" that we will study in this lesson with the understanding that there is more that could be said, and more we are still learning about this particular style Healing Prayer. But "Inner Healing Prayer" is an expression of ministry that is rooted in the concepts of God's salvation and God's peace which we studied in the previous lesson. All forms of Healing are only made possible because of Jesus.

The goal of all Healing Prayer is not just "the act of healing," but how all forms of healing should always point back to Jesus Christ and His victory for us over the power of sin and death.

Let's begin with ...

A Definition Of Inner Healing

Francis MacNutt has been involved in the ministry and study of Healing Prayer since 1967. In his book "Healing," often used as a textbook in seminaries, he expresses his thoughts on inner healing as follows:

"The idea behind inner healing is simply that we can ask Jesus Christ to walk back to the time we were hurt and to free us from the effects of that wound in the present. This involves two things: 1) Bringing to light the things that have hurt us, 2) Praying to ask the Lord to heal the binding effects of the hurtful incidents of the past." (page 147, "Healing," by Francis MacNutt)

Can you think of ways that events from someone's past might keep them from moving forward in their life? From having a greater sense of freedom in life?
_____
_____
_____
_____
_____

Can you think of ways that "past hurts" might affect current relationships?
_____
_____
_____
_____
_____

www.DennyFinnegan.com

Can you think of ways that the issue of "forgiveness" might prevent a person's gaining greater peace in Jesus Christ? From obtaining a greater release into Jesus' salvation?
_____
_____
_____
_____

What are some of the reasons, then, that someone may need Inner Healing?
_____
_____
_____
_____

The issue of forgiveness plays a prominent role in Inner Healing Prayer - to forgive or to be forgiven. I have personally experienced, in both prayer for myself and in prayer for others, how Inner Healing may often lead to Physical Healing. As Francis MacNutt also writes, "Forgiveness [is] the most important form of repentance" (page 137, "Healing," by Francis MacNutt).

Let's look at some specific examples of how Jesus brought Inner Healing to people through prophetic insight which the Holy Spirit gave to Him - sometimes it was in the form of prayer; sometimes it came as a pronouncement or command.

Jesus Heals A Paralytic

Read John 5:1-9 together.

This man had been disabled *"for 38 years"* (vs.5)! Why do you think Jesus asked him, *"Do you want to get well?"* (vs.6)?
_____
_____
_____
_____

What might be some of the *"anger issues"* this man was dealing with inside? Some of the *"forgiveness issues"* (vs.7)?
_____
_____
_____
_____

The man was healed by Jesus physically. But how might Jesus' question and command also have brought to him Inner Healing?
_____
_____
_____
_____

Jesus Heals A Sick Woman

Read Luke 8:43-48.

According to Leviticus 12:4-5, and Leviticus 15:25, this woman was *"unclean"* and anything - or anyone - she touched would become *"unclean."* She was especially prohibited from entering the sanctuary of God and from touching *"any consecrated thing"* - especially a Rabbi or Prophet of God.

So, what might be some of her reasons for *"sneaking up"* on Jesus? For *"sneaking away"* from Jesus?

_____
_____
_____

What might be some of her Inner Healing issues? (e.g. forgiveness, angers, hurts, feelings of rejection, shame, fears, etc...)

_____
_____
_____

What are some of the reasons Jesus did not want to leave her Physical Healing *"anonymous?"*

_____
_____
_____

In verse 48, Jesus said to her, *"Daughter, your faith has healed you. Go in peace."* What might have been some of the Inner Healing she received along with the Physical Healing?

_____
_____
_____

Jesus Heals Through Forgiveness

Read Luke 7:36-50 together.

Jesus connects our *"sense of need for forgiveness"* to how we treat others, how we love, and how we sense we are loved by God and by others.

How did the Pharisee's "sense of need for forgiveness" affect his treatment of Jesus? of this woman?

_____
_____
_____

www.DennyFinnegan.com

How did this woman's "sense of need for forgiveness" affect her treatment of Jesus?
_____
_____
_____

In verse 48, Jesus prophetically pronounces, "Your sins have been forgiven." What might be some of the ways she received Inner Healing?
_____
_____
_____

Small Group Discussion

1) What did you learn about Jesus' reasons for healing people?

2) What did you learn about our reasons for praying for healing?

Small Group Prayer Exercise

In this prayer we are going to combine the practice of what we have learnt in the preceding lessons with the principles revealed in this lesson. (Note: One of the ways the Holy Spirit might guide you with a "word" could be through a Scripture verse that applies to the situation.)

1) Ask for a volunteer who is willing to be prayed for by the group.

2) One of the class leaders will be the "Point Person" for this time of prayer - they will "moderate" how the prayer will take place for the volunteer.

3) Together, ask the Holy Spirit to show you how the Lord would have you pray for the volunteer ... then listen to the Lord. Here, we are expecting the Lord to give some or all either "words of knowledge," "words of wisdom," or words related to "discernment of spirits." (From Lesson 8.)

4) The "Point Person" will wait until they sense the Lord leading them to ask you for any "words" the Holy Spirit may be revealing to those in the class.

5) Before praying these "words," the "Point Person" will "test them" with the volunteer. Don't worry if you do not have a sense of anything; or even if you may have been off target. The purpose of the exercise is to "become more experienced through practice".

6) Confirm the "words" through "testing them" (Four Tests from Lesson 8). Then the "Point Person" will lead the time of prayer for the volunteer, with the rest of the class "praying in agreement" as the Holy Spirit leads.

LESSON 12 : PHYSICAL HEALING

Should we pray for Physical Healing?

As we start this lesson, I believe it is very important that we begin with the heart of Jesus for people. One of the verses in the Bible that reveals a lot about the heart of Jesus also happens to be the shortest verse in the Bible: *"Jesus wept."* (John 11:35). In this passage from John 11, Jesus is reacting to the pain and grief He felt for Lazarus' death, and for Martha's and Mary's grief over the death of their brother Lazarus. Even though Jesus was only moments away from raising Lazarus from the dead, *"Jesus [still] wept."*

A second verse that demonstrates that Jesus did what He did from His Heart of Love is Matthew 9:36, *"When he saw the crowds, he had compassion on them, because they were harassed and helpless, like sheep without a shepherd."* The word "compassion" could probably be translated as "gut-ache."

Jesus ministered to people, first and foremost, because Jesus cared about the people to whom He ministered! And every time Jesus demonstrated the salvation and shalom of God in His ministry to them, He was revealing the Heart of God for them ... the Love of God for them.

Jesus has commissioned and empowered us to pray for *"signs to accompany"* our proclamation of Him (cf. Mark 16:15-18). And both Jesus and the Apostle Paul makes it clear that the teaching and preaching of Jesus is to be accompanied *"with power"* (cf. Matt.10:5–8; Luke 9:1-2; 10:1-2,17; Rom.1:4; 1 Cor.1:17;2:4; Eph.3:16; 1 Thess.1:5). But our primary reason for *Why We Pray for Physical Healing* is to imitate Jesus... to show others *"the love of God that is in Christ Jesus our Lord"* (Romans 8:39). Anyone remember John 3:16?

Reasons Jesus Healed And Why We Should Pray For Healing

1. Read Matthew 8:5-13.

Why did Jesus heal this person?
___
___
___
___

How did it demonstrate the salvation of God? the peace of God?
___
___
___
___

www.DennyFinnegan.com

What impact might this healing have had upon the centurion? Upon those who witnessed this?

_____
_____
_____
_____

2. Read Luke 7:18-23:

What does Jesus say are His reasons for healing?

_____
_____
_____
_____

How did it demonstrate the salvation of God? The peace of God?

_____
_____
_____
_____

What impact might His healing(s) have had upon those who witness it?

_____
_____
_____
_____

3. Read Luke 5:20-26:

Why did Jesus heal this person?

_____
_____
_____
_____

How did it demonstrate the salvation of God? The peace of God?

_____
_____
_____
_____

What impact might His healing(s) have had upon those who witness it?

_____
_____
_____
_____

FOUNDATIONS - Understanding Prayer Ministry

4. Read Luke 9:1-2; 10:1-2:

What authority and power did Jesus give when He sent out His followers?
_____
_____
_____
_____

How would the power and authority Jesus gave them demonstrate that the kingdom of God was breaking into their world?
_____
_____
_____
_____

How did it demonstrate the salvation of God? The peace of God?
_____
_____
_____
_____

What impact might their healing(s) have had upon those who witness it?
_____
_____
_____
_____

Small Group Discussion

1) What did you learn about Jesus' reasons for healing people?

2) What did you learn about our reasons for praying for healing?

Small Group Prayer Exercise

In this prayer exercise, we are going to combine the practice of what we have learned in the preceding lessons with the principles revealed in this lesson.

1) Ask for a volunteer who is willing to be prayed for by the group.

2) One of the class leaders will be the "Point Person" for this time of prayer, and will "moderate" how the prayer will take place for the volunteer.

3) Together, ask the Holy Spirit to show you how the Lord would have you pray for the volunteer ... then listen to the Lord. Here, we are expecting the Lord to give (some or all) "words of knowledge," "words of wisdom," and/or words related to "discernment of spirits"
(From Lesson 8).

4) The "Point Person" will wait until they sense the Lord leading them to ask you for any "words" the Holy Spirit may be revealing to those in the class.

5) Before praying these "words," the "Point Person" will "test them" with the volunteer. Don't worry if you do not have a sense of anything; or even if you may have been off target. The purpose of the exercise is to become more experienced through practice.

6) Confirm the "words" through "testing them" (Four Tests from Lesson 8). Then the "Point Person" will lead the time of prayer for the volunteer, with the rest of the class "praying in agreement" as the Holy Spirit leads.

LESSON 13 : FREEDOM IN CHRIST

How do Christians join Jesus in praying for Freedom In Christ?

The type of Healing Prayer we are about to discuss is considered controversial. It is a style of Prayer Ministry that is also called "Praying for Deliverance." What makes this controversial are the varying view points on whether or not a Christian can be "possessed." The main Greek word used for this concept better translates as "demonized," and does not necessarily imply "possession." I believe the meaning of this concept can be found in Jesus' own words in a healing He performed in the Gospel of Luke 13:10-16:

"10 On a Sabbath Jesus was teaching in one of the synagogues, 11 and a woman was there who had been crippled by a spirit for eighteen years. She was bent over and could not straighten up at all. 12 When Jesus saw her, he called her forward and said to her, "Woman, you are set free from your infirmity." 13 Then he put his hands on her, and immediately she straightened up and praised God. 14 Indignant because Jesus had healed on the Sabbath, the synagogue ruler said to the people, "There are six days for work. So come and be healed on those days, not on the Sabbath." 15 The Lord answered him, "You hypocrites! Doesn't each of you on the Sabbath untie his ox or donkey from the stall and lead it out to give it water? 16 Then should not this woman, a daughter of Abraham, whom Satan has kept bound for eighteen long years, be set free on the Sabbath day from what bound her?"

Here we see clearly that Jesus believed this woman's illness was a work of Satan. It connects to Jesus' stated mission in Luke 4:18-19: *"to proclaim freedom for prisoners"* or to *"release the oppressed."*

What types of fears might be generated from the truth that Satan is the source of a person's illness?
_____
_____
_____
_____

What hope in Christ is generated from Jesus' healing in this passage?
_____
_____
_____
_____

How is this type of Healing a demonstration of God's salvation? Of God's peace? Of God's love?
_____
_____
_____
_____

Now, we are going to look at three passages that will help us better understand *How Christians Join with Jesus in Praying for Freedom in Christ*". They are: 1) Acts 16:16-18; 2) Acts 19:13-17; 3) Luke 8:26-39.

How Do Christians Join With Jesus In Praying For Freedom In Christ?

1. Read Acts 16:16-18:

Where did Paul's power and authority to cast this *"spirit"* out of her come from?

_____
_____
_____
_____

Was her message true? What was wrong with her message?

_____
_____
_____
_____

Why do you think the Holy Spirit inspired Paul to cast this *"spirit"* out of her?

_____
_____
_____
_____

2. Read Acts 19:13-17:

According to verse 14, why were these *"seven sons of Sceva"* unable to set this man free from these evil spirits?

_____
_____
_____
_____

Where did Paul's authority and power to *"drive out evil spirits"* come from? Where did Jesus' authority and power come from?

_____
_____
_____
_____

Even though they were unable to *"drive out evil spirits"* from this person, Jesus still received glory and honor. *Why?*

_____
_____
_____
_____

3. Read Luke 8:26-39:

What condition was this man in as a result of being *"held in captivity"* to these evil spirits (vs.27-29)? of being set free from these evil spirits (vs.35,39)?

_____
_____
_____
_____

How is this type of Healing a demonstration of God's salvation? of God's peace? Of God's love?

_____
_____
_____
_____

What hope in Christ might be generated from Jesus' healing in this passage?

_____
_____
_____
_____

How was the Kingdom of God advanced through this Healing Prayer?

_____
_____
_____
_____
_____

Small Group Discussion

1) What did you learn about Jesus' reasons for healing people?

2) What did you learn about our reasons for healing people?

Small Group Prayer Exercise

(Same exercise as in Lesson 12)

1) Ask for a volunteer who is willing to be prayed for by the group.

2) One of the class leaders will be the "Point Person" for this time of prayer to "moderate" the prayer.

3) Invite the Holy Spirit to show you how the Lord would have you pray for the volunteer ... then listen to the Lord.

4) The "Point Person" will wait until they sense the Lord leading them to ask you for any "words" the Holy Spirit may be revealing to those in the class.

5) Before praying these "words", the "Point Person" will "test them" with the volunteer.

6) Confirm the "words" through "testing them" (Four Tests from Lesson 8). Then the "Point Person" will lead the time of prayer for the volunteer, with the rest of the class "praying in agreement" as the Holy Spirit leads.

Prayer Journal

Date: Prayer Need: Date Answered:

_____

_____

_____

_____

_____

_____

_____

_____

_____

_____

_____

_____

_____

_____

_____

_____

_____

_____

_____

_____

www.DennyFinnegan.com

Prayer Journal

Date:	Prayer Need:	Date Answered:

www.ingramcontent.com/pod-product-compliance
Lightning Source LLC
Chambersburg PA
CBHW041552220426
43666CB00002B/41